RECIPE FOR OUTLINING

A Fun & Flexible Guide for Planning Your Novel

Megan Barnhard

Recipe for Outlining: A Fun & Flexible Guide for Planning Your Novel
© 2018 Megan Barnhard.

Megan Barnhard
www.MeganBarnhard.com

Printed in the United States of America

First Printing: June, 2018

For all the writers I've coached over the years. Thank you for being brave enough to share your process and your creativity with me and for being my guinea pigs.

TABLE OF CONTENTS

Getting Started..1
Chapter 1: The Biggest Myths About Outlining.............................. 6
Chapter 2: The Massive Benefits of Outlining 12
Chapter 3: Plan of Attack...18
Chapter 4: Finding Your Outlining Style 22
Chapter 5: Mission Statement... 34
Chapter 6: Central Conflict 38
Chapter 7: Conflict Map..46
Chapter 8: Anchor Scenes 55
Chapter 9: Story Stepping Stones 64
Chapter 10: Scene Planning..71
Chapter 11: Putting It All Together 77

    How Far Ahead Should I Plan?.. 78
    How Detailed Does My Outline Need to Be?.............................. 78
    I Don't Know What to Write Next. What Should I Do?............... 79

Chapter 12: Reflect & Take Action... 82
Acknowledgements... 85
About the Author 86
More By this Author 87

GETTING STARTED

You

You are an author. Whether you've written dozens of books or you're embarking on your very first one, you know that you were meant to write stories and share them with the world.

You've always loved getting lost in your creativity. But you may not always have had a reliable way to go from *great idea in your brain* to *finished story on the page.*

Creativity keeps its own schedule. Sometimes it overwhelms us with flashes of insight. Other times, it stays away for so long we're left wondering what we did to offend it. It might strike at the most inconvenient times. Creativity doesn't care if we're trying to catch up on laundry or work emails.

As an author, your beautiful challenge is to take those flashes of creative insight and get them down on paper, one chapter at a time, without losing your ideas. And that's no easy feat.

That's where outlining comes in. An outline is a plan that helps you go from great idea to finished draft, even in the midst of your busy life.

What's your personal history with outlining?

Maybe you've never tried outlining because it reminds you of your horrible 7th grade English teacher who made you use Roman numeral outlines for EVERYTHING. Maybe you've dabbled in different kinds of outlines but never found one that really made organizing your thoughts easier. Maybe you're a dedicated pantser, feeling like outlines would just slow you down and annoy your muse.

The funny thing is that outlining—when done right—actually enhances creativity. It gives you more freedom and flexibility. It helps you manage all the great ideas that spin around in your brain. And it ensures that those ideas actually make it onto the page so you can publish them.

When you find the kind of outline that speaks to your inner organizer, you'll be writing stories faster and with more joy. You'll be able to stay in the creative flow longer. You'll ditch writer's block and improve your story crafting skills.

Sound hard to believe? I see it with my own eyes all the time.

Me

I'm a writing coach. I've been running my own business helping writers since 2006. Before that, I was a classroom teacher. And long before that, I was an eager writer.

When I was young, I loved writing. Words flowed through me and I lived in language. I wrote poems, reflections, and stories.

As long as I could get them out in one draft.

If I couldn't finish a project in one single burst of creative energy, it didn't get finished. If I walked away from a piece of writing, it was over. Has that ever happened to you?

When I started writing essays in college, I was in over my head. My practice of turning in last-minute word-vomit first drafts wasn't going to cut it. Fortunately, because of the program I was in, I couldn't get around writing. I had to get through it.

I started visiting the student writing center and talking to the volunteers. They would ask me about my ideas, and I realized that this was an entire part of writing I had been skipping: the planning part. I'd just been jumping into drafting without gathering my ideas or figuring out how to arrange them so they made sense.

That's how I learned about the writing process.

Once it was revealed to me, I was hooked. It led me to wanting to know how brains and words work together—and how they don't. I studied multi-sensory teaching techniques and learned tons of strategies for helping writers plan, draft and revise with less frustration.

From there, it was only a few short steps to my career as a writing coach.

Now, I help entrepreneurs and creatives tame the writing process and tell their stories. I guide them through the steps of writing—planning, outlining, drafting, revising, editing, and publishing—and help them find the techniques, shortcuts, and hacks that make writing easier and more enjoyable.

So, when I talk about what works, I don't just mean for me. I mean for the hundreds of writers I've worked with who came from different backgrounds and had different thinking and learning styles.

Coaching all those writers showed me that there's no one way to outline. When I use the term "outline" I really mean any system you can use to clarify and organize your ideas.

I don't believe in outlining for the sake of outlining. I don't make my clients (or myself) write down more than is needed to recall the thought later while drafting.

Having a good outline is like having a playlist made so you can keep dancing, rather than stopping after each song to think about what song you want to hear next. It keeps the momentum (and the party) going.

So, let's get this party started.

This Book

This book is a peacemaker. It ends the war between your creative muse and your inner deadline setter. It brings peaceful coexistence to your writing flow and your commitment to get your books published and selling. It also declares a truce between plotters and pantsers. You don't have to choose a side when it comes to writing your novels.

When you learn how to outline in a way that works for you, you'll be able to maximize your creative flow and stay in "the zone" longer, which means you'll be more productive and efficient. Your creative brain will feel free and uninterrupted, and your analytical brain will meet your deadlines and allow you to sell books. Win-win!

If you're a dedicated panster, this book will help you plan your writing in flexible ways while maintaining that "seat of your pants" thrill.

If you're a die-hard plotter, this book will help you plan smarter and in stages so that you don't waste time and energy over-planning.

Here's what we'll be doing in this book.

First, I'm going to walk you through the biggest myths about outlining and show you how you might be doing more work than you need to when you sit down to outline. My goal is for you to work smarter, not harder, so it's important to show you some common misconceptions about outlining. Once we've cleared up those myths, we'll look at the benefits of outlining.

Then, we'll go through different brainstorming and outlining techniques so you can find an approach that works for you.

After that, I'm going to break down the different stages of outlining one at a time, show you how to use them, and tell you exactly when and where in your writing process they will be the most helpful. We'll look at writing recipes you can use at each stage, as well as examples from some well-known stories so that the ideas feel concrete, rather than abstract.

At the end of each chapter, you'll find a Chapter Check In so that you can pause and take stock of the info we've covered. My goal in providing these sections is to help you apply the material by reflecting on your insights, questions, and plans for implementation.

CHAPTER 1: THE BIGGEST MYTHS ABOUT OUTLINING

Myth #1 Outlining Is Only for Linear Thinkers

The truth: There's an outlining style for every type of thinker.

Don't be embarrassed if you've bought into this myth. A lot of creative people do. They look at an outline for a novel—the bullet points, graphic organizers, whiteboard full of notes, storyboard, etc.—and think, "My brain is not that organized!"

But the way an outline looks and the way it's built are very different, just like a book itself.

Outlining is a multi-step process. It's a system that includes capturing ideas, ordering them based on story structure, and then figuring out how to store them in a way you can use as you're drafting.

Think of outlining as:

1. Gathering your ideas
2. Organizing your ideas
3. Writing down your ideas as a set of instructions you can follow as you draft, aka a writing recipe

If you've always been put off by outlining, I'm guessing you were trying to do all three of these key steps at the same time. That's a tall order, and it can feel pretty overwhelming.

"Gathering ideas" looks different for each author. Your creative process might be linear, or it might be random, explosive, and beautifully chaotic. Maybe you dream about scenes or characters. Maybe you feel like a muse is working through you. Awesome! You don't have to give that up in order to outline. When done strategically, outlining actually supports your creative process because it focuses your energy and effort.

Once you've gathered your ideas, you'll need to organize them and figure out the order in which they'll appear in your novel. This won't require a lot of big thinking from you, though, because good stories follow a predictable structure. There's no need to reinvent the wheel; simply use the story structure covered in this book to ensure that you have a clear beginning, middle, and end, and that your story has all the elements readers will expect.

Following standard story structure makes the writing process smoother and more enjoyable since you're spending less time making decisions and more time being creative.

Finally, the way you capture your ideas and turn them into a writing recipe will be personalized to your thinking style. I encourage you to fill out the Planning Questionnaire to discover how you tackle big projects. (You'll find a link to it and to all the other outlining resources I refer to in this book at the end of Chapter 3.)

Here's an example of what that little questionnaire can do.

I worked with a writer this year who was really struggling with outlining, feeling unsure of the right order of events in her story. She had thought a ton about her novel. She knew her characters really well. She knew how she wanted things to end. But the plot was a bit murky in her mind.

She'd tried moving from Point A, to Point B, to Point C, but she was coming up dry. As soon as she tried to plan in this linear way, she couldn't come up with a single idea she liked.

After filling out the Planning Questionnaire, she had a huge A-ha! moment: She could use her experience as an interior decorator in her writing. She "designed" a bunch of individual scenes she knew she wanted. Each scene was inspired by her initial vision for the book and had its own coherence, like the mood boards she would have used to plan a home design. Since she didn't have to worry about how they connected, her creativity flowed.

Once she had several of these scenes designed, she started arranging them like puzzle pieces to see how they fit together to tell the story.

Her final outline was a circle, with her central conflict in the center and her key scenes arranged in "slices" going clockwise around the circle. It was one of the coolest outlines I had ever seen, and unlike anything I ever would have suggested or thought of. I love that by giving herself permission to use her strengths, this writer found an outlining style that totally worked for her. Once she had this outline, she finished the first draft of her novel in about a quarter of the time it had taken her to write her previous novel.

Myth # 2: You Must Outline the Whole Story Before You Start Writing

The truth: Outlining is an on-going process.

It's pretty much impossible (and also really uninspiring) to do all the planning for your whole story before you start writing. Has that been holding you back? Did you feel like you had to pay your planning dues before you were even allowed to start writing your story? That's the opposite of motivating. The reason you got into authoring was because you wanted to write stories, right?

In addition to being a drag, doing all of your outlining before you draft creates tension between your planning brain and your inspired brain. This is why so many writers resist outlining: they want to leave space for the wonderful ideas that pop up without warning.

I bet you've had the experience at least once of a fantastic idea just popping into your brain as you write. Without warning, you find yourself writing a brilliant sentence, plot development, or line of dialogue. I see this happen to authors all the time, and it's one of the best parts of being a writing coach. The big secret is that this kind of magical moment is a lot more likely to happen when you outline in stages.

A few years ago, I worked with a young writer who was writing an adventure story. She had the key steps in her plot planned out but she wasn't feeling very excited or directed. There seemed to be too many choices about how her protagonist could get from the introduction of the conflict up to the crisis moment in the climax.

During one of our sessions, as she was drafting a scene, one of her characters suddenly did something unplanned and unexpected.

In that moment, this writer gasped with delight. She realized that this minor character would be the perfect vehicle for introducing an element of the conflict that had been missing: She had wanted her main character to get to act like a spy, using tech and gadgets to investigate the weird stuff happening in his life. The minor character was a hacker and opened up a world of possibility.

This is the kind of gift you can give yourself if you leave some gaps in your outline and figure out the details while drafting.

As you can see, there's room for both planning and inspiration when you outline in stages rather than all at the start. This approach to outlining also helps you fight back against the two big bad P's of writing: procrastination and perfectionism.

Doing all the planning at the beginning can actually be a form of procrastination. It's a chance for the little fears inside our brains to say, "I can't possibly start writing yet! I haven't outlined what my characters will eat for breakfast every day." Planning is less risky than doing. If you're nervous about getting your writing out into the world—and we've all been there—staying in the planning zone can feel more comfortable. Arm yourself against this kind of procrastination by outlining in stages.

Trying to plan every detail of your story before you begin writing can also trigger feelings of perfectionism. There are many details you won't be able to foresee from the start. This is a good thing! It means you'll have space for your characters to make organic decisions. If you try to anticipate all the details that will arise, you might find that you get stalled by trying to think of the absolute best outcome, plot device, character development, etc.

There's no such thing as a perfect unfolding of your story; there's only the way you feel called to tell it. Unless you're a Mozart type who can hear the entire orchestra in your head and what every instrument should be doing at every moment, you're going to have some surprises in your own story. The reality is that you'll keep adding to and refining your outline as you draft. Which brings us to the next myth.

Myth # 3: An Outline is Set in Stone

The truth: You're allowed to change your mind about your story.

The key is that if you leave your old plan behind, you need to make a new plan. Jump in and change your outline. Cross stuff off. Switch out characters and places. You are doing yourself a huge favor.

The best storytellers evaluate their stories as they go and make the changes they need to along the way.

Let go of the myth that an outline locks you into one course of action. Instead, embrace the idea that your outline is your map, and if you decide you want to go somewhere different, you need a new map for that destination.

One of my favorite outline-changing stories involves another young author who was writing a horror novel. Her main character was a delightfully sardonic anti-hero named Elliott.

Leading up to the climax of the story, Elliott has a big blowout with his buddy Drew, a supporting character. Her original plan called for a make-up scene between the two friends to explain why Drew would show up to help Elliott in the climax.

The make-up scene was a can of worms: Including it would mean including several additional scenes. First, Elliott would have to see the error of his ways, then there would have to be a scene explaining why Drew would agree to meet up with Elliott after their big fight. To make matters worse, the argument occurred as the story approached its climactic scene , so inserting additional scenes would have killed the tight pacing and tension.

We paused to reassess the outline. When this writer had initially planned her story, Drew had been the voice of reason. But as she'd written this character, he'd become more of the rescuer. The enabler. He was constantly bending over backwards to help Elliott, despite the latter being a needy jerk. It was actually more realistic for the main character *not* to apologize, and for his friend to show up to bail him out anyway.

With this insight, she made a simple and quick change to her outline by deleting the plan for the "can of worms" scenes. If she had waited until she revised, she would have ended up drafting two full chapters and then cutting them. This way, she cut the extraneous scenes and then planned an easy transition into the two characters meeting up in the climax. Not only did she keep the great tension, she also made her characters more believable.

Chapter Check In
- Any Aha! moments in this chapter?
- Which of these myths have you been buying into?
- Which other myths or limiting beliefs about your own writing process have you been holding onto?
- Do you feel ready to let go of these myths?
- What's something you want to try adding to your Author Toolbox now that you've read this section?
- What questions came up?

CHAPTER 2: THE MASSIVE BENEFITS OF OUTLINING

Once you stop believing the common myths around outlining, you're free to discover what outlining means to you and how you can make it work for your thinking style and your story. You're also perfectly positioned to cash in on the big benefits of outlining.

Benefit 1: Write a Story Readers Love

A good novel doesn't just happen. If you want to write a story readers love, you need quality ingredients mixed together in the right amounts.

As humans, we're surrounded by stories. We watch stories on TV and in the movie theater. We hear stories from our friends and families, and we cry over videos of heart-warming stories on social media. All this exposure to stories makes us experts about them.

That means no matter what genre you write, your readers have certain expectations for your story. They may not realize they have these expectations or be able to name them out loud, but by golly, they'll sure as heck be able to tell the whole world how unsatisfied they are if you fail to meet those expectations!

The good news for you as an author is that a good story follows a formula. A recipe. If you learn that recipe and follow it, you'll be on the path to writing a story that readers will love.

I'm going to give you the basic recipe below. There will be some extra ingredients you need to include for your particular genre (more about that when we talk about mission statements), but all good stories need the following ingredients:

- A main character we relate to who goes on a journey (it doesn't have to be a literal journey).
- An interesting central conflict introduced in a believable way.
- Mounting drama as the conflict unfolds.
- A climactic scene that makes us feel satisfied because the main character faces exactly what she needs to in this scene, whether it's a baddie, a decision, or some part of herself she's been avoiding.
- A resolution to the conflict, even if there's no happy ending.

Using these ingredients in the right order is the difference between a story that readers love and one they don't even finish reading.

Benefit 2: Find More Time to Write

If you constantly find yourself wishing you had more time to write in the midst of your busy life, outlining will completely change your writing practice.

First, when you know you have a plan, you'll be more motivated to sit down and start writing. Procrastination will lose its luster because you'll know exactly what you're avoiding doing. Washing the dishes instead of writing might seem like a good idea. But washing the dishes instead of writing the scene in the tavern that will set up the climax and leave you only eight chapters from the end of your book... Not as easy to justify, right?

Additionally, a good outline lets you get more done in a shorter amount of time. Imagine being able to bust out the rough draft of a scene in the time it takes the washing machine to do a load of laundry because you've already mapped out exactly what needs to happen.

Working from an outline boosts your efficiency in other ways, too. Having a solid outline helps you focus on the elements of your story that are the most important. You'll write fewer scenes that are brilliant but end up being cut because they're detours or tangents.

Finally, when you follow the outlining process in this book, you'll stave off the big time-suck so many authors fear: writer's block. Writer's block occurs when we come up against obstacles or difficult choices in the story. This book will show you reliable techniques for making decisions and overcoming obstacles so that you maximize your writing time and minimize your "blocked" time.

Benefit 3: Stop Editing Your Story to Death

The more you plan your story, the less you have to rewrite it. Time spent planning versus time spent revising is not an even trade. Revising and editing are the most time-consuming and dangerous parts of writing.

You heard me right: dangerous.

Editing, revising, and rewriting are the places where it's easy to start completely unraveling your novel. It's like pulling on a little thread on your sweater and all of sudden finding you've pulled out an entire sleeve! It happens insanely quickly and the results are devastating. The structure will be gone and you'll find yourself wondering what the heck your story was about and why on Earth you thought you were capable of writing one. I'm not exaggerating.

Smart outlining also saves time during the drafting stage because it prevents you from writing a lot of material that you ultimately won't use. Outlining helps you plan larger elements before details so that you're sure the details fit your story.

Imagine the frustration of writing a brilliant description, only to realize later that the event doesn't work in the narrative. Instead, it ends up on the cutting room floor.

The outlining process in this book takes you from bigger to smaller, beginning with a foundation that will hold up the rest of your story.

When it is finally time to edit your draft, you'll be able to check each chapter and scene against its purpose, as defined by your outline. That means you won't cut key scenes or mess up the order of events. Having a clear plan when you're editing makes the difference between finishing and giving up.

Benefit 4: Actually Finish Your Book

If you don't know your final destination and the path you'll take to get to it before you begin drafting your novel, it's easy to end up muddled in the middle or writing yourself in circles.

When you're running on pure momentum and you hit a dead-end, it's frustrating. For a lot of writers, it's enough to make them stop writing completely.

In contrast, having a good outline means you don't have to give up when inspiration runs dry. Your outline tells you where you're going. Once you know that, you can problem-solve on the way to get there. You can brainstorm about options based on the next key event you know needs to occur in the story. From there, you can check in with your writing buddies or a coach to ask which option seems the most believable or interesting. But the choices are contained, not endless. You can approach things from your problem-solving brain rather than your Ack!-I've-got-to-be-brilliant brain.

Benefit 5: Stop Wasting Energy by Over-Writing

Sometimes we write too much. We want to make sure that a character's motivation is clear. Or a backstory is sound. Or a unique feature about the world makes sense. So, we explain it in painstaking detail. Then we worry it's still not clear, and we explain some more. Having an outline is your protection against this. When you look at all the pieces in a finished first draft, you'll be able to make a more informed decision about whether you need to add more detail, description, or explanation.

Of course, once you've got a draft, you can also ask an early reader to let you know whether things are making sense. Join a writing group, find a coach, or make friends with other writers online.

The problem with writing yourself down a rabbit hole of extra explanation or sub-sub-sub-plotlines is that it can steal your writing momentum. Imagine all the creative energy that you should be using to advance the plot getting hijacked by a long explanation of why elephants are used as the primary source of transportation in the setting of your novel.

I can tell you from personal experience that this is no fun. In my twenties, I made a film with some friends. It was supposed to be a drama about cowboys. It was supposed to be a love story. It was supposed to be good.

When my writing partner and I worked on the script, we kept worrying about whether the audience would get why characters were doing what they were doing. Would their motivation be clear? Would people understand the backstory? Would the audience know enough history for the story to make sense?

Each doubt led to more rewrites. We kept adding more and more explanation. The script was taking so long to write that I lost interest. I just wanted it to be finished, so I phoned in the most important parts: the drama and the love story. What should have been the climactic scene ended up as an epilogue. D'oh!

The finished movie was little more than a series of close-ups of characters explaining who they were and why they wanted what they wanted. It was awful.

We had meandered so far into exposition territory that the movie didn't even have a plot.

If we'd had an outline, we could have seen that we were spending way too much time on unimportant scenes and that the drama, tension, and romance were getting lost in the shuffle. If we had worked from bigger tasks to smaller tasks, we also would have seen that the movie was missing a central conflict and character arcs.

You'll get a chance to see why those elements are so important in upcoming chapters. But I bet you can imagine how boring a western is when all characters do is talk about what they've done. It was like watching the characters from *Deadwood* go to therapy.

Chapter Check In
- Any A-ha! moments from the chapter?
- Which of these benefits have you been missing out on? How do you feel about that?

- Which benefit are you most looking forward to getting?
- What's something you want to try adding to your Author Toolbox now that you've read this section?
- What questions came up?

CHAPTER 3: PLAN OF ATTACK

Writing is like cooking. It's a creative and messy experience full of experimentation. And the whole thing goes a lot smoother and yields better results if you have a plan close at hand that tells you the key ingredients you need and how to put them together.

This book will help you create and use writing recipes so that you can draft with greater ease and inspiration.

As you saw when we debunked those three myths, outlining works best when you do it in stages. The process I'll show you takes you through six key stages:

1. Mission Statement
2. Central Conflict
3. Conflict Map: Character Arc & Plot
4. Anchor Scenes
5. Story Stepping Stones
6. Scene Planners

You also learned that the process of outlining has three key steps:
- Gathering your ideas
- Organizing your ideas and putting them in order
- Turning your ideas into instructions, aka writing recipes, you can refer to as you write

I'll show you how to complete each of those steps, offering tips for different thinking styles.

Since you're going to be working in stages and creating several different writing recipes, make sure you have a way to keep track of them all that feels streamlined and convenient for the way you think and work. Here are some suggestions:
- Print all your recipes/write them out by hand and store them in a binder.

- Use poster board or a big whiteboard to create a giant plot hill and use index cards or sticky notes to add chapter notes to the part of the story where they belong.
- Type up all your recipes, put them in a Google Doc or a Word Doc, and save them to the cloud.
- Use a planning software, such as Asana, Trello, or Monday, to create different boards for different parts of your outline.
- Use your favorite author software.

I personally use Google Docs to store all of my recipes in a Planning Doc. I can always print an individual recipe if that makes it easier to draft from, but there are some nice advantages to having my outline recipes in Google Docs:

(1) Google auto saves docs to the cloud every few seconds. Not only does this mean I have a built-in back-up, it also means I can write from anywhere and even access my recipes from my phone.

(2) Speaking of my phone, I love using Google Keep, a note-taking app that captures text, voice-to-text, images, and audio recordings. It's really easy to turn content from a Keep note into a Doc or add it to an existing Doc. I'll often find myself needing to walk away from the computer to clear my head when I'm struggling with big ideas. I usually walk around my front yard talking to my phone using the voice-to-text feature of Keep. The fresh air and the movement get my thinking going, and I can easily add all my good ideas and big questions to my Planning Doc.

(3) I can easily capture freewrites, character studies, or random scenes I've written and see where they fit into my outline.

Let's say I did a freewrite about a key setting in my story, just as an exercise to think through how I could describe it. I came up with some details that I'd really like to use and that I think would draw the reader into the world I've created. I will copy and paste the relevant parts from that freewrite into my Planning Doc so that I don't forget about them when it comes time to draft that section.

I dump this kind of material into the spot where I think it could go, but I don't stress over exactly where I put it. In fact, I even create a section at the bottom of my Planning Doc called "Storage" so that I can add elements and ideas even when I've got no idea where they go. That's as low-pressure as it gets.

(4) I can easily share my Planning Doc with someone else for feedback. (I ask my writing coaching clients to use Google Docs so that we can literally be on the same page.) It's easy for us to see one another's updates in real time, as well as collaborate, comment, and create to-do lists.

If a Planning Doc sounds like it's right for you, try using the template I've included in the Outline Recipes Bundle at the end of this chapter. I encourage you to modify it and make it work for you, but the template will give you a place to start.

Even if you're really eager to take action, I recommend you read the next chapter, "Finding Your Outlining Style." That's where you'll find suggestions for coming up with your best ideas. This a step we often forget, and technically it's not outlining; it's brainstorming. It's the fun part where you get to play Mad Scientist and come up with lots of cool, creative ideas.

That chapter is also where you'll find insights about different thinking styles and which types of brainstorming work well for them. The more you know your own thinking style, the more efficient and effective you'll become at brainstorming and outlining.

Once you've read about outlining styles, you can choose your own adventure moving forward. If you're eager to start your outline immediately, use each section of this book as you outline your novel. If, on the other hand, you like to get the big picture before getting started, read all the way through and then come back to each chapter when you're ready to use it.

However you tackle this material, make sure to take some time to answer the questions in the Chapter Check Ins. This will help you process the information and think about how you can apply it to your writing process, whether you take action right then or wait to get the lay of the land first.

When you find activities that work for you, add them to your Author Toolbox. That's your treasure chest of strategies and techniques that you've found helpful for your writing process. Track what works for you as well as what doesn't. Try out different techniques and experiments. You'll up-level your craft and use your time more efficiently by turning helpful techniques into habits.

I've put together a bundle of all the outlining templates I talk about in the book, including an Author Toolbox and Planning Doc Template, so that you can have your very own copies to use. You can download the Outline Recipes Bundle at meganbarnhard.com/outline-recipes

CHAPTER 4: FINDING YOUR OUTLINING STYLE

There are two big questions to ask yourself in order to discover your outlining style:

(1) How do I get my best ideas?

(2) How do I like information arranged so that I can act on it?

It's important to give your ideas time and space to bubble up from that deep and fertile pit of creativity in the bottom of your soul. But you don't have to come up with your ideas in a vacuum. Structure and formulas can spark your creativity.

Since stories follow a reliable structure, you don't have to reinvent the wheel when it comes to planning your novel. Instead, you can focus on finding reliable methods of jumpstarting your creativity so that it gives you the answers to specific questions you ask it.

You might already have some tried-and-true methods for coming up with great ideas. Yay! If not, or if you'd like more, you'll get a bunch in this chapter.

We'll start by looking at the layers of brainstorming.

3 Brainstorming Approaches

If I ask you why Dorothy didn't make it into the storm cellar before the tornado hit, you could answer in a few different ways.

You might say it was because Toto ran away so she had to rescue him. Or, you might say it's because Dorothy is at the beginning of her arc and is still impetuous and immature, so she has to demonstrate this by acting without thinking. Or, you could say it was because she had to be in the house when it got picked up by the twister, otherwise the rest of the events in the plot wouldn't occur. All three answers are correct.

There's a lot that goes on in any given scene of your novel. There's the action happening. There's also the emotional state of your character—how she's developing as a person on her arc. Plus, there's all the cool behind-the-scenes stuff that creates drama and tension.

When you brainstorm about your story, you can do it at any of those three levels: plot details, character arcs, behind-the-scenes stuff, or even a combination of all three. It really depends on what pops into your head first and what you feel best guides you as you write.

Here's what the same chapter of a novel would look like using each approach:

Approach #1: Using Plot Details
1. Event 1
2. Event 2
3. Event 3
4. Event 4
5. Event 5
6. Event 6

Example
1. Effie & Olivia talking on train
2. Commotion—woman notices a theft
3. E & O worried they'll be found out as orphans
4. E & O run
5. E & O catch attention of police
6. E & O escape in crowded train station; helped by kind stranger

Approach #2: Using Character Arc/ Emotion Details
1. Character motivation → Action → Consequence
2. Character motivation → Action → Consequence
3. Character motivation → Action → Consequence

Example
1. Olivia fed up with Effie → leaves her alone → conductor spots Effie
2. Effie mad at being treated like a baby → disobeys her sister somehow → nearly gets them caught

3. Effie wants attention → does her "cute" act for strangers → the strangers help them somehow

Approach #3: Using Behind the Scenes Details
1. Inciting incident
2. Meet antagonist
3. Establish backstory
4. Establish what's at stake
5. Meet first ally

Example
1. Inciting incident: police look for thief; girls must get off train
2. Antagonist: conductor calls police
3. Backstory: establish E & O are orphans
4. At stake: they have to run to avoid being separated
5. Meet first ally: someone in train station who will help them

(The number of items in these outlines isn't fixed; use as many as you need.)

Notice that #1 shows what the characters will do. This is a helpful way to outline if you naturally think in scenes or details.

On the other hand, #2 has a lot of unknowns—notice the use of "somehow." This is a great way to outline if you prefer to think in concepts and character motivation and don't mind working out the details as you write.

#3 is a behind-the-scenes look at the chapter, reminding you, the author, where you are in the story. This is a great way to outline if you naturally think in terms of plot structure, OR if you often find yourself lost in the details and you want to make sure you're staying focused on the most important aspects of each chapter.

Keep these approaches in mind as we look at different styles of planning.

Six Common Thinking Types

Read through each planning style and ask...
- Does it sound like you and how you think?
- Have you used it to help you create a story in the past?
- Can you imagine it working for you?

Bottom-Up Thinkers

You collect interesting moments and then tie them together into scenes or stories. You can imagine exactly how your protagonist looks as he stares forlornly into his cup of Earl Grey at the funky-smelling cafe with the broken air conditioner and the tattooed barista. But you're not sure why he's there or what this scene is for.

Brainstorming Techniques for Bottom-Up Thinkers
- Jot down ideas for scenes on notecards, sticky notes, or in a notebook whenever they come up.
- Freewrite about your characters and get clear on who they are and what they want.
- Brainstorm about what to put in a scene, focusing on characters' actions and their logical consequences, e.g., Jim would get sick, so he would miss the meeting, so Brad would get the account, so Jim would get further depressed, so Rhonda would have an excuse to leave him.
- Freewrite about a character, setting, event, scene, or plot point you want to get clarity about.
- Make a mind-map of the scenes or events you know you want to include. See what ideas for scenes arise from these.

Writing Recipes for Bottom-Up Thinkers
- Arrange your index cards or sticky notes in the order that you want them to appear in the story.
- Copy and paste your notes or bullet points into your Planning Doc in the order you want them to appear in your story.

Top-Down Thinkers

The *why* is more important than the *what* for you. You know the purpose and the reason for your characters and your scenes. You might write with placeholders, knowing that in Chapter 5 Ted has to meet someone who will push him to take a risk, but you don't know who that person is or what that risk will be. You'll figure out the details when you get there.

Brainstorming Activities for Top-Down Thinkers
- Write down the following terms on separate pieces of paper and brainstorm possible scenes for each one:
  - Beginning of conflict
  - Tensest moment of conflict
  - Resolution of conflict
- Brainstorm what to put in a scene focusing on "behind-the-scenes" details, e.g., Jim has to do something that will make Rhonda mad.
- Brainstorm what to put in a scene focusing on emotional beats and how your characters' motivations would lead them to act, e.g., Rhonda wants to prove her superiority, so she would sabotage something important to showcase her own skills.
- Make a mind-map of all your characters and the conflicts and allegiances that connect them. See what ideas for scenes arise from these relationships.

Writing Recipes for Top-Down Thinkers
- Highlight the ideas you like best from your brainstorms about the beginning of the conflict, the tensest moment of the conflict, and the resolution of the conflict. Type these into your Planning Doc and add in details as you come up with them.
- Create descriptive chapter titles in your Planning Doc in the style of an old-timey book. For example, Chapter 4: In Which Percy Realizes He Is Not a Normal Kid. You don't have to keep these chapter titles; they're just placeholders for you as you write.

- Paste your emotional beat brainstorms into your Planning Doc next to their corresponding chapter headers or scene titles.
- Paste your "behind-the-scenes" brainstorms into your Planning Doc next to their corresponding chapter headers or scene titles.

Associative Thinkers

One idea leads you to the next. You love the feeling of "flow" when characters seem to act of their own accord and tell you what they should do next. You can get lost in writing for hours and completely surprise yourself with the ideas that arise.

Brainstorming Activities for Associative Thinkers
- Freewrite for at least 10 minutes at the beginning of each planning session. See what ideas come up and where you might use them.
- Freewrite about a character, setting, event, scene, or plot point you want to get clarity about.
- Make a mind-map of the scenes or events you know you want to include. See what ideas for scenes arise from these.
- Talk your story through with other people and bounce ideas off them.
- Write out a summary of your story. Don't plan ahead; just let it flow and see what happens.
- Brainstorm what to put in a scene focusing on emotional beats and how your characters' motivations would lead them to act, e.g., Rhonda wants to prove her superiority, so she would sabotage something important to showcase her own skills.
- Make a mind-map of all your characters and the conflicts and allegiances that connect them. See what ideas for scenes arise from these relationships.

Writing Recipes for Associative Thinkers
- Mind-map your scenes and color-code them to show which scenes center around different characters, settings, or themes.

- Mind-map your scenes and color-code or arrange them to show the chronological order of scenes.
- Take your mind-map of characters and their conflicts and number the events in the order in which they'll occur in your story.
- Color-code your freewrites according to events, characters, or themes, then copy and paste the different colors into different sections of your Planning Doc.

Big Picture Thinkers

You need to be able to zoom out and see the big picture. Too many details slow you down and make you feel overwhelmed or impatient. You like graphic organizers, and arranging ideas from top to bottom or left to right on the page helps you orient yourself. You love knowing where it's all going. You can see the finish line even from the start. You have a clear vision but can sometimes get bogged down in the details or run into writer's block for individual chapters.

Brainstorming Activities for Big-Picture Thinkers
- Make a mind-map of the scenes or events you know you want to include. See what ideas for scenes arise from these.
- Write down the following terms on separate pieces of paper and brainstorm possible scenes for each one:
    - Beginning of conflict
    - Tensest moment of conflict
    - Resolution of conflict
- Brainstorm what to put in a scene focusing on "behind-the-scenes" details, e.g., Jim has to do something that will make Rhonda mad.
- Brainstorm what to put in a scene focusing on emotional beats and how your characters' motivations would lead them to act, e.g., Rhonda wants to prove her superiority, so she would sabotage something important to showcase her own skills.

Writing Recipes for Big-Picture Thinkers

- Create descriptive chapter titles in your Planning Doc in the style of an old-timey book. For example, Chapter 4: In Which Percy Realizes He Is Not a Normal Kid. You don't have to keep these chapter titles; they're just placeholders for you as you write.
- Create a circle outline with the central conflict in the center and each key scene as a "slice" of the circle.
- Create a mind-map with the central conflict in the middle and scenes clustered around it. (There's a mind-map template for you in the Outline Recipes Bundle.)

"Know it When I See It" Thinkers

You tend to feel limited by outlines. You don't want to commit to a particular plan because you know some brilliant idea is just around the corner. You're inspired by details, able to fill an entire page describing the look of an object or a character's expression.

Brainstorming Activities for "Know it When I See It" Thinkers

- Freewrite about a character, setting, event, scene, or plot point you want to get clarity about.
- Talk your story through with other people and bounce ideas off them.
- Write down each of the anchor scene names (see Chapter 8) on a separate piece of paper and brainstorm possible scenes for each one.
- Write out a summary of your story. Don't plan ahead; just let it flow and see what happens.
- Tell your story out loud. Record it.

Writing Recipes for "Know it When I See It" Thinkers

- Highlight the ideas you like best from your anchor scene brainstorms. Type these into your Planning Doc and add in details as you come up with them.

- Create scene titles or chapter headers in your Planning Doc. Copy and paste the various possibilities you're considering for each section. Put your favorites in bold but keep the other ideas there as a reminder of WHY you're using the events you've chosen.
- Create scene titles or chapter headings on a whiteboard or a piece of big poster paper. Jot down the various possibilities you're considering for each section on the whiteboard, or on sticky notes. Once you pick "winners" move the other ideas down to a storage area so that you can use them in other places if you like.

Linear Thinkers

Skipping around drives you nuts. You like moving from Point A to Point B, and only then figuring out Point C. You are very logical, using what you see in your plan or your draft to help you move naturally to the next scene or chapter.

Brainstorming Activities for Linear Thinkers
- Tell your story out loud off the top of your head. Record it.
- Brainstorm what to put in a scene focusing on characters' actions and their logical consequences, e.g., Jim would get sick, so he would miss the meeting, so Brad would get the account, so Jim would get further depressed, so Rhonda would have an excuse to leave him.
- Use stepping stone tables to think through "which leads to..." and "which would have happened because..." to generate both causes and effects. (You'll find templates for this in the Outlining Recipes Bundle.)

Writing Recipes for Linear Thinkers
- Create descriptive chapter titles in your Planning Doc in the style of an old-timey book. For example, Chapter 4: In Which Percy Realizes He Is Not a Normal Kid. You don't have to keep these chapter titles; they're just placeholders for you as you

write. Put these chapter titles on a timeline on a whiteboard or big sheet of poster paper.
- Add a bulleted list of events under each chapter in your Planning Doc.
- Create a storyboard.
- Put all your scenes or chapter headings on index cards or sticky notes and put them in order.

How Does Your Brain Work?

Before we leave behind this section about how you think and plan, it's worth mentioning that the categories above barely scratch the surface of all the different kinds of thinkers there are.

Brains are wired in lots of different, wonderful, fascinating ways. This means there are a ton of different ways we process and recall information. A lot of modern media is geared toward people who are visual and auditory. That means information, from the classroom, to the boardroom, to social media is presented for us to see and hear.

Not everyone is a visual or auditory thinker, though.

Have you ever marched in place while trying to memorize something or had to perform an action yourself before you could describe a character doing it? If you've always felt like you don't absorb things when you see or hear them, you might be a kinesthetic thinker and at your sharpest when you get up and move your body.

You can use kinesthetic thinking in your outlining process. Get up out of your chair. Take a walk, bounce in place, dance. Act out scenes. Talk to yourself. Pace as you brainstorm. Invite friends over and roleplay your characters. (Or do it alone. Who cares what your cat thinks?)

When you're ready to build recipes, use your body. Write out scenes on a whiteboard. This big writing engages more of your muscles—your whole arm and shoulder, and your legs if you stand while doing it—and will fire more neurons than writing small on a piece of paper.

Write out scenes on notecards or sticky notes, and then use your body to pick them up and move them where they need to go in your story.

Build a model or map of your setting and place sticky notes or board game pieces where key scenes will happen.

For kinesthetic thinkers, moving is like an extra dose of oxygen or caffeine: it focuses and motivates you.

You might see yourself in more than one of these thinking and planning styles. They're not exclusive categories. Labeling yourself is not important. Instead, try out the methods and ideas that appeal to you or sound fun. These are the ones that will most likely work with your brain.

Keep an experimental mindset and play with various techniques until you find the ones that work best for you.

When you have success with a technique, keep track of it! Add it to your Author Toolbox so you can keep using it. A full Author Toolbox is like money in the bank. It helps you write books more efficiently. You'll stop wasting time on what doesn't work. You'll be able to jumpstart your creativity and repeat the process. That's what will open up the road to being a professional author: having repeatable systems that work.

Here's the most important message of this chapter: **You need to find recipes you can write from.** They don't have to make sense to anyone else; they just have to work for you.

Want to go even further? Consider...
- Hand-written vs. on the computer
- Notes vs. full sentences
- All in one spot vs. divided into several mini-outlines
- Arranged spatially? (sticky notes, index cards, storyboarding, whiteboard with each scene pointing to the next)
- Arranged linearly? (chapters in order from top to bottom or left to right)
- Arranged associatively? (mind-map)
- Arranged by character? (color coded, character cards)
- Analog? (binder with one page for each writing recipe)

- In the order of the story or the order in which you're planning to write?

Chapter Check In:
1. Any A-ha! moments from this chapter?
2. Do you see yourself clearly in any of these thinking styles? Do you see an overlap of some of the categories?
3. Do you think you're a kinesthetic thinker?
4. Which 2-3 brainstorming techniques will you try first?
5. Which writing recipes do you think will work for you? Why?
6. Anything to add to your Author Toolbox?

CHAPTER 5: MISSION STATEMENT

It's time to jump into the six stages of outlining. This first stage might seem like overkill. A lot of authors skip it. More accurately, it never occurs to them to do this.

A lot of authors also give up halfway through their books. Coincidence? Nope.

The first stage of outlining is creating a mission statement for your project.

What a Mission Statement Does

A mission statement—whether it's for a book or a business—lays out your BIG PURPOSE. You can look to that statement when you don't know what to do next. It keeps you on track.

Your big purpose for your book includes your motivation. Your big WHY. Your reason for writing.

When you're really clear on why you're writing this specific book, you'll be much more likely to stick it out through the hard parts. Instead of giving up, you'll pull out your Author Toolbox or get help from a coach or writing community.

I worked with an author recently who had lost steam while revising. (This happens to a lot of writers because revising is hard.) She was struggling with the mechanics, but she was really clear on her reason for writing: a powerful theme she wanted to showcase in the novel. When current events began eerily mimicking the situations in her book, she was immediately motivated to redouble her editing efforts and get some help so that she could get her book—and her message of hope—out to the world. That's the power of a mission statement.

On a practical level, you'll also be able to solve problems more easily. You'll have a framework for answering the questions that arise about what should happen next in your story.

That's because your mission statement includes a lot of on-the-ground details, such as...

- Genre and subgenre
- Length/Number of Chapters
- Tone & Writing style
- Mood
- Narrative POV and Style
- How you want readers to feel at the end of the story

When to Make a Mission Statement

The best time to create your mission statement is at the beginning, before you start drafting. But, as the old proverb about planting trees goes, the next best time is now.

How to Build a Mission Statement

Brainstorm and research answers to the questions below. You can write your answers on a piece of paper or use the mission statement template in the Outline Recipes Bundle.

Step 1: What type of book are you writing?

- Genre and subgenre.
- Approximate length: number of words or number of chapters. (A simple search online will tell you average lengths for all types of genres.)
- Narrative style and voice, e.g., first person from the POV of the 12-year-old protagonist, close third person following the two main characters, omniscient.
- Tone and mood, e.g., humorous, poignant, suspenseful, spooky, fun, lighthearted, dramatic, wacky, intense, absurd, thrilling, sad.

Step 2: Why are you excited about this book?
- Why do you want to write this book?
- Is there a character or type of character you want to showcase?
- Is there a world or setting you want to explore in great detail?
- Is there a theme or message you want to express to readers?
- Is there an audience you really want to reach?
- What are your marketing or income goals for this book?

Step 3: What are your must-have elements?
- "Books in my genre really need to have..."
- "My book won't feel complete without..."
- "I'm really looking forward to my book including..."

Step 4: What are your literary pet peeves?
- Characters who do/don't...
- Settings that do/don't...
- Conflicts that do/don't...
- Climaxes that do/don't...
- Resolutions to conflicts that do/don't...
- First scenes that do/don't...
- Final scenes that do/don't...
- A writing style that does/doesn't...

Step 5: How would you like your readers to react?
- "I hope they'll have a deeper appreciation of..."
- "I hope they'll have a better understanding of..."
- "I hope they'll feel..."
- "I hope they'll want to..."

Mission Statement Recipe

I want to write a [Step 1 Answers] book that centers around [most important elements of Step 2]. It will include [Step 3 Answers]. It will avoid [Step 4 Answers]. It would delight me if readers walked away thinking/feeling [Step 5 Answers].

Don't worry about making your mission statement sound good. It can be a laundry list. You can even leave it as bullet points or notes if that feels more useful. You might prefer an image or a set of symbols for your mission statement.

Whatever your mission statement looks like, put it somewhere you can see it as you write: the top of your Planning Doc, taped up on the wall in your writing space, or as the desktop image on your laptop.

Example Mission Statement
The Dancing Cats Compete
I want to write a 12,000–15,000-word middle grade chapter book set in an imaginary world but driven by real emotions, actions, and reactions. It will center around friendship, social struggles, and battling perfectionism. Talking animals with human traits will demonstrate themes related to growth, navigating conflict, and courage.

I want to speak to highly-sensitive young people and help them examine the fear of failure. There will be several design challenges throughout the book to encourage readers to create writing, art, or movement related to the experiences of the characters. It will avoid being preachy and pedantic while still delivering a clear theme about the need for patience for self and others. There should be moments of humor, pathos, tension, and silliness.

I would be delighted if kids and adults alike walked away feeling touched by the friendship between Tabbi and Calica and inspired to continue the conversations about perfectionism and facing fears. Readers should also laugh at the antics of Uncle Hank and want to get up and dance when they read about Calica's triumphant solo.

Chapter Check In:
1. Any A-ha! moments in this chapter?
2. What questions did this chapter bring up for you?
3. Any additional information you need to gather before you can write your mission statement?
4. What are your next steps?

CHAPTER 6: CENTRAL CONFLICT

The second stage of outlining is determining your central conflict. This tells you who wants what, why, and why it's so hard to get.

What Your Central Conflict Does

Conflict is what drives your story. Without a strong and well-defined central conflict, it doesn't matter how vivid your descriptions are, how fascinating your main character is, or how gritty and real your dialogue is. Without a conflict, there's no story.

A conflict arises when a character wants something and can't get it immediately. The story is everything that happens between the wanting and the getting (or the not getting but ceasing-to-want for some other reason).

Your central conflict is also the track that keeps your story moving in the right direction. Just as your mission statement will give you momentum if your motivation starts to dwindle, your central conflict will save your bacon if your plot starts meandering or getting convoluted.

When to Build Your Central Conflict

Build your central conflict after you create your mission statement and before you do any other "plotting"—before you start figuring out the details of who's going to do what, when.

Whatever your central conflict is, it needs to be inspiring—not only to readers, but to you, the author! The reason you'll keep writing is because you care about your central conflict. You care about showing readers what happens when someone who wants X tries to get it by doing Y while being opposed by Z.

Not only is your central conflict your inspiration for writing, it's also a clear map of where your story is going. It shows you where your main character begins, where she ends up, and the toughest thing she has to face along the way.

Once you know your conflict, your story is going somewhere. And not just somewhere. Somewhere *interesting*!

Sometimes a fantastic central conflict will simply pop into your brain, as if your muse sent it to you by mental text. But not always. That's why I want to walk you through how to build a captivating central conflict one step at a time.

We'll go through three strategies for building your central conflict: using a character, using a setting, and using a theme or message. Try whichever method grabs your attention, or try them all and use the results you like the best.

Protagonist-Inspired Conflict

Step 1: Brainstorm Key Traits

Brainstorm possible key traits for your main character. These might be any of the following, or combinations of them:

Traits:

- Occupation/vocation
- Skills and hobbies
- Goals and dreams
- Greatest fear
- Secret desire
- Greatest strength
- Major flaw(s)
- Powers and abilities
- Mindset
- Accident of birth
- Formative experience
- Unique perspective
- Convictions/beliefs

Examples:

- A shy boy with a lightning scar who survived the attack of a powerful wizard. (the Harry Potter series)
- A Puritan minister in love with the woman whose child he secretly fathered. (*The Scarlet Letter*)
- A young woman who, due to being the youngest daughter, is never allowed to fall in love or get married. (*Like Water for Chocolate*)
- A young man whose parents are murdered in front of him when he's a small boy, making him obsessed with justice. (*Batman*)

Step 2: Explore the Traits

Pick one key trait at a time and imagine several likely actions and results for it. For each trait, write down what a character with that trait would be likely to do or not do, and then the potential conflict that could arise from that action or inaction. You might find a table like this helpful for organizing your ideas:

Trait	Action or Complication	Resulting Conflict
Parents murdered in front of him when he's young; engenders a deep hatred of criminals.	Obsessed with justice → becomes a vigilante wearing a bat costume.	Goes around fighting crime, but since he doesn't reveal his true identity, the powers that be think he's a baddie. He has to go after criminals without being caught by the police himself.

(*Batman*)

Protagonist-Inspired Central Conflict Recipes

- [MC with trait] wants/needs to [objective or goal] but can't get it until she overcomes [obstacle] by [action/choice].
- [MC] struggles with [trait] until she overcomes [obstacle] by [action/choice].
- [MC with trait] is opposed by [antagonist or circumstance] until she overcomes [obstacle] by [action/choice].

Protagonist-Inspired Conflict Example

A young boy is manipulated by a mutinous pirate he secretly respects until he overcomes his gullibility and need for a father figure and stands up for himself. (*Treasure Island*)

Setting-Inspired Conflict

Step 1: Brainstorm Settings

Brainstorm some possible settings that interest you. These might be any of the following, or combinations of them:

- City
- Region
- Country
- Historical era
- Historical event
- Future era
- Future event
- Community
- Set of circumstances

Example Settings

- A world in which time travel exists.
- An era where the United States has split up into individual states or regions.
- The time of the Spanish conquistadors.
- Paris during World War II.
- A small family farm in rural Appalachia during the Depression.

Step 2: Explore the Settings

Pick one setting at a time and for each one, write down the dangers and tensions that would be present. Then, imagine a specific conflict that might arise from these circumstances. You might find a table like this helpful for organizing your ideas:

Setting	Action or Complication	Resulting Conflict
Dystopian future. After years of war, a tyrannical government rules all known planets. Space travel has created "Wild West" conditions where outlaws can live on the fringe of civilization.	A group of former rebels can't accept defeat and continues the insurrection by smuggling and breaking the laws of the space empire on their salvage ship.	They need passengers to make a living, but passengers pose great threats: They compromise the captain's renegade values, are potential snitches, or are outlaws even more dangerous than the crew itself.

(*Firefly*)

Setting-Inspired Conflict Recipes

- MC wants [goal] but can't get it due to [circumstance of setting]. In order to [goal], she'll have to confront [most dangerous aspect of setting].
- Due to [circumstance of setting], MC finds herself facing [opportunity/obligation]. In order to [goal], she'll have to confront [most dangerous aspect of setting].

Example Setting-Inspired Conflict

Due to the invention of a vast network of technology that eventually enslaves humanity, a young woman must stop a killer robot from destroying her so that she can give birth to a son who will go on to liberate humanity. To survive, she must trust a time traveler and use her wits and strength to outrun and outsmart the perfect killing machine. (*The Terminator*)

Theme-Inspired Conflict

Step 1: Brainstorm Themes

Brainstorm some themes that interest you. When readers finish your story, how should they be affected?

- Question or doubt something?
- Believe in something?
- Understand or empathize with a type of person?
- Want to take action or change something?

Use the list that follows to get your ideas going. Ask yourself what message you'd like to demonstrate about one of these topics or about a combination of them.

- Being a good person
- Justice
- Revenge
- War/violence
- Peace
- Love
- Honesty
- Loyalty

Examples of themes:

- Everyone will betray you in the end.
- Love is more powerful than hatred.
- Sometimes justice must be tempered by mercy.
- Hard work pays off.

- We can never escape our destiny.
- Nice gals finish last.

Step 2: Explore the Themes

A theme arises when we see the outcome of a circumstance and a specific choice. Should you take a nap during the race, or should you keep plodding along? Ask the tortoise. Should you be nasty and rotten, or should you treat every living creature—even mice—with kindness? Ask Cinderella. Should you build a slapdash house and then go play, or should you take the time to build a solid structure? Ask the three little pigs.

For each theme you consider, brainstorm a circumstance, a choice, and an outcome you could use to demonstrate the message you want to impart. You might find a table like this helpful for organizing your ideas:

Circumstance	Choice	Outcome	Message
A hare challenges a tortoise to a race that seems impossible for the tortoise to win.	The tortoise keep moving, doing his best, and ignoring the hare's taunts.	After the over-confident hare stops to rest, the tortoise wins the race.	Slow and steady wins the race.

(Aesop's Fables "The Tortoise and the Hare")

Theme-Inspired Conflict Recipe

MC finds herself [circumstance beyond MC's control]. When she decides to [action], it leads to [outcome], showing that [message].

Example

Meg Murry, who has always felt dumb and boorish compared to her father and brother, finds herself traveling through time and space to rescue her father. When she learns to control her anger and stop trying to prove herself to others, it leads to her rescuing not only her father, but her younger brother, whom she thought was smarter than her in every way, showing that there are different kinds of strengths. (*A Wrinkle in Time*)

Chapter Check In:
1. Any A-ha! moments from this chapter?
2. What questions did this chapter bring up for you?
3. What kind of central conflict do you think will work for you: one based on character, on setting, or on theme? What modifications, if any, will you need to make?
4. Anything to add to your Author Toolbox?
5. What are your next steps?

CHAPTER 7: CONFLICT MAP

Whether you built a protagonist-inspired, setting-inspired, or theme-inspired central conflict, the next stage of outlining is to create a map of that central conflict. You'll draw your conflict map using two key sources of information: a plot hill and a character arc (or multiple character arcs if you have multiple main characters).

What a Conflict Map Does

A conflict map shows you the beginning, middle, and end of your central conflict so that you can plan the specific events that will occur. It's made up of two smaller pieces: a plot hill, which shows the action and events that occur, and a character arc, which shows how your main character is affected by those actions and events.

It's true that there are some books we read just for the plot, just as there are some movies we see only for the special effects.

Most of the time, though, we need something more.

We need a character whose story we care about. When you overlay a character's arc, aka her emotional journey, on top of the plot, you draw your readers deeper into the story and make them fall in love with your characters. Writing a series? This is especially important! You need readers to want to come back and hear more about these same characters.

A great example of the relationship between plot and character arc comes from *Star Wars: A New Hope*. Life, freedom, and the destiny of the galaxy are at stake, but in that climactic moment, we don't just care whether the Death Star is destroyed; we care whether Luke destroys it using the Force, thus showing that he has matured and learned to trust himself.

Character arc is the same as character development: It's the journey a character goes on internally. A character can go on a journey even if she never leaves home. It's not how far she travels that's important, but how much she learns. Wrestling with the challenges of the central conflict should cause your main character to grow and change.

The plot hill is the obstacle course that allows characters to demonstrate their flaws, growth, and eventual mastery or failure. As characters navigate this obstacle course, they experience challenges and triumphs while also demonstrating their key strengths and weaknesses. As their journeys end, we see how they have grown and changed as a result of what they've been through.

When you overlay the character arc on the plot hill, you get your story map.

Plot Hill

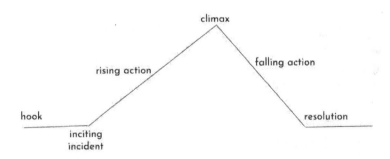

An incident early on sets off the rising drama, leading up to a moment of maximum tension, and then falling drama, or a cool-off period, leading to the ultimate solution to the conflict.

Character Arc

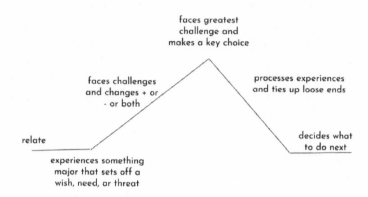

Near the beginning, something occurs that forces the main character into action. It makes her want or need something specific and have to work to get it; alternatively, it introduces a threat the main character has to confront.

The rising slope indicates mounting challenges that propel the main character forward toward the ultimate climax point, where she has to deal with the conflict head on. In this scene, she'll have to face something she doesn't want to face and make a key decision about the conflict she's been embroiled in up to this point.

Following the climax, she processes what she's been through so that in the resolution she can decide what to do next.

A Note About Multiple Main Characters

Build a separate character arc for each of your main characters. Think of the first Harry Potter book: Hermione, Ron, and Harry each grow and change in different ways over the course of the novel, exhibiting flaws and growth as they make their way toward the climax.

If your characters work together, you'll want a single climax where each character can demonstrate growth or overcome a challenge. This doesn't have to be a single scene, but if it's a series of scenes, they should all be connected and happen in succession.

Grouping characters' crisis moments together makes it easier to curate the moments of tension and relief for your readers. In the first Harry Potter book, Hermione, Ron, and Harry display great skill in the climax of the story as they battle plants, play the ultimate game of chess, and face off against Professor Quirrell, who's being controlled by Voldemort. Even though each character has a chance to demonstrate unique skills, the drama and action are contained to a few chapters.

If you have multiple characters who don't follow the same plot hill, you'll not only need to build separate arcs for each but potentially separate plot hills as well. If they start out apart but come together at some point, you can draw plot hills that begin separately and combine as the story or series progresses. Think of Lyra and Will from the *His Dark Materials* series by Philip Pullman.

It is possible to have multiple main characters who don't meet at all in a story because they are going to meet and either help or oppose one another in a later book in the series. You'll need to create entirely separate arcs and plot hills for such characters. Even so, their respective climactic moments should arrive in close sequence to consolidate the drama.

A Note About Supporting Characters

Supporting characters can have their own arcs as well. These mini-arcs and whatever mini-plot hills you create for them can fit into the larger plot hill(s) of your main character(s), for example, somewhere on the rising action slope.

You can use those character journeys to take a break from your main narrative and make readers wait for the results of an important development in the main plot. These mini-detours are subplots that add depth and drama to your story.

When to Build Your Conflict Map

Create your conflict map after you've zeroed in on your central conflict and before you start drafting. You want to use only the plot hill(s) and arc(s) of your main character(s). Hold off on adding in the arcs and plot hills of any supporting characters until you have your big picture.

How to Build Your Conflict Map

Select the type of conflict you're using and brainstorm answers to the questions. If you need help coming up with ideas, don't forget about all those brainstorming techniques I showed you in Chapter 4.

Character-Inspired Conflict

1. How will the trait be revealed, the power be received, or the circumstance be brought to a decision point?
2. What key choices would naturally grow out of this character's situation?
3. What gets the story going? What event or occurrence would force this character to take charge of her situation?
4. What is this character's greatest fear?
5. What big choice will your character have to make? What turning point will she arrive at? How will the key trait force some kind of action with high stakes?
6. What will your protagonist achieve at the end? How will the problem get resolved? Will it be over or just paused? Why? How? Who will act?

Setting-Inspired Conflict

1. In your setting, who has power, and who is the underdog? Why? (Hint: Underdogs make great protagonists!)
2. What are the most important/potentially dangerous circumstances and features of this setting?
3. How could these circumstances and features be used for and against people?

4. What gets the story going? Will there be a major change that occurs in the setting? Will hidden circumstances be revealed? Why is today different from yesterday?
5. Who will the protagonist be? What will this person be trying to do to escape or change the setting?
6. What big danger could the protagonist face? What would be terrifying to face or satisfying conquer?
7. What could happen to the protagonist at the end? Why? How? How might this affect other characters?

Theme-Inspired Conflict
1. In your setting, who has power, and who is the underdog? Why? (Hint: Underdogs make great protagonists!)
2. Who will the protagonist be? What will this person's circumstances be at the start of the story? What circumstances will provide the biggest obstacle or opportunity?
3. Who or what is in opposition to this protagonist? Why or how does this person, group, circumstance, or idea cause the protagonist to act?
4. What gets the story going? Will there be a major change that occurs? Why is today different from yesterday?
5. What big danger could the protagonist face? What would be terrifying to face or satisfying to conquer?
6. What key decision could the protagonist make to demonstrate her beliefs in relation to the theme?
7. What could happen to the protagonist at the end to reinforce the theme?

Writing Recipes

Protagonist-Inspired Conflict Map

Climax:
a choice must be made
and the key trait comes
into play

Inciting Incident:
trait revealed; power
received; circumstance
discovered

Resolution:
protagonist attains
goal, changes goal,
or can no longer
pursue goal

Setting-Inspired Conflict Map

Climax:
protagonist faces most
dangerous aspect of
setting or symbol thereof

Inciting Incident:
event; change in setting or
circumstance

Resolution:
protagonist leaves
setting; setting no longer
dangerous; immediate
threat resolved

Theme-Inspired Conflict Map

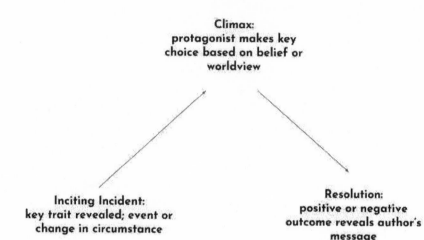

Climax:
protagonist makes key
choice based on belief or
worldview

Inciting Incident:
key trait revealed; event or
change in circumstance

Resolution:
positive or negative
outcome reveals author's
message

Chapter Check In

1. Any A-ha! moments in this chapter?
2. What questions did this chapter bring up for you?
3. Do you need more clarity about the journey and motivation of your protagonist(s)?
4. Do you need more clarity about the three core points of your plot: the beginning of the action, the most dangerous moment, or the end?
5. Anything to add to your Author Toolbox?
6. What are your next steps?

CHAPTER 8: ANCHOR SCENES

OK, time for a metaphor switch. Up to now, we've been talking about building a foundation for your story and cooking with recipes. Now, I want you to stop thinking about your story for a bit and start thinking about *the process of writing the story.*

Writing a book is like trying to cross a raging river. It's not possible to jump all the way from one bank to the other. You need some rocks to step on. Good news: you've got a crane and access to a stone quarry.

The next stage of outlining is to start dumping big boulders into the river of your writing, which will do two, things:

(1) Slow the rushing pace of the river, making it easier for you to cross; and

(2) Give you sturdy platforms to stand on so you can take things one step at a time.

The boulders you're going to drop into this raging river aren't simply platforms to stand on, though. They're special and specific. They work directly in the service of your plot hill and your character arc and help you create what I call anchor scenes—the scenes that help you tell a great story. These special scenes anchor your story to the most important elements of effective narrative structure.

What Anchor Scenes Do

Writer's block might look like sitting down and staring at the blank page, feeling totally uninspired. Or it might look like avoiding sitting down in the first place. That pile of laundry or all those work emails suddenly seem really important. In my experience as a writer and a writing coach, though, about 90% of writer's block is caused by not knowing what is supposed to happen next.

Anchor scenes are an amazing defense against writer's block and procrastination as well. As you're crossing that wild writing river, being able to see the next big boulder to jump to makes all the difference—even if it's a pretty big jump away from where you are right now.

Anchor scenes give you destinations. And as long as you have your next destination, you can plan your route. If you can see the next big boulder, I promise you that you can get to it. (We'll cover more about how to do this in the next chapter.)

Anchor scenes are also insurance against random rambling. If you've ever gotten muddled in the middle of your story or had no idea what should happen next, anchor scenes are the solution.

They're not just for you, though. Even if it were somehow possible for you as the author to jump from one side of the writing river to the other, it wouldn't make for a good story. If readers only cared about the end, they wouldn't read the book; they'd just read a summary.

Your readers want a story that has a beginning, middle, and end, makes sense, and says something interesting. Remember, a great story isn't just a lot of action; it's a character going on a journey. The anchor scenes in your story help your readers *experience* your story rather than just hear about it.

Anchor scenes take readers through various levels of thinking and feeling. They allow readers to connect with characters, settings, and themes. They include all the big ingredients of story structure: inciting incident, rising action, climax, falling action, and resolution.

I'll walk you through creating the core anchor scenes that all stories need, but do your homework about your genre. A comedy needs different key scenes than a tragedy does. A space opera has different destinations along its plot and character arc than a cozy mystery or a paranormal romance.

Before creating your anchor scenes, return to the planning and research you did when you created your mission statement so that you know all the must-have elements of your story in mind.

When to Build Anchor Scenes

Plan your anchor scenes after you've created your conflict map. You'll need to know your central conflict and where your main character is going to end up, plus the outline of the big challenge she's going to face in the climactic scene.

Remember that there are different approaches to brainstorming, as you saw in Chapter 4. It's perfectly fine if you don't know the details of what's going to happen in your story. You might know the general shape of things instead. For example, I might have an anchor scene that looks like this: *Some kind of fight between Lucy and Tigue so that when they go to explore the woods they decide to split up.* I know that these two characters have to split up, but I don't know why or how.

That means don't wait until you're clear on absolutely everything before you create your anchor scenes. Instead, treat your anchor scenes like a sketch: Get down as much of the shape as you can and fill in the "color" and "shading" later.   It's alright if you're kind of fuzzy on the details. What's most important is actively thinking about these key ingredients of your story.

Heck, even just asking yourself what your boulders will be puts you on the path to crossing the river because it makes you actively look for the events you need to build your story.

How to Build Anchor Scenes

After you've built your conflict map, use what you know about plot hill and character arc, plus your mission statement and what you know about your genre, to create your anchor scenes.

Below you'll find expanded descriptions of the key points of the plot hill and character arc you saw in Chapter 7. Take some time to read through them and determine whether you need to do any additional research about how these elements are supposed to appear or be used in your genre.

I recommend jotting down some notes or ideas in response to the questions and bullet points so that you can capture your ideas as they arise.

Hook/Relate

Grab readers' attention and get them invested in your main character right from the beginning. Give readers a way to relate to your main character through a vulnerability of some kind.

Inciting Incident/Wish, Need, Threat

Start the conflict by introducing your MC's objective. Your MC does/experiences something that sends her on a new path.

What's different now that this incident has occurred? Why is this conflict happening now? What got it all started? Why is today different from yesterday?

- Meeting someone new (friend or foe)
- Natural/man-made disaster or accident
- New information
- Betrayal/revelation of true intention
- Change of setting: time, place, circumstance
- Trait, power, or true identity revealed

Rising Action/Challenges & Changes

Show your MC working toward her objective. Create smaller problems along the way to solving the main conflict. Help readers continue to bond with the main character by revealing more flaws, weaknesses, strengths, blind spots, and obstacles.

Build the tension and make readers wonder whether the main character will ever reach her objective. Utilize subplots to introduce key traits of your MC, build and relieve tension, and delay reveals.

Along the journey, your main character(s) will face smaller conflicts. These might be related to the central conflict, or they might be independent:

- Smaller battles in a larger war
- A series of unrelated obstacles
- Multiple manifestations of the same problem
- Universe out to get you
- Consequences of decisions

- Collecting skills
- Collecting other characters
- Trying and failing
- Getting a little bit stronger over time
- Two steps forward, one step back
- Pushed toward a breaking point
- Collecting clues to solve a mystery

Climax/Greatest Challenge & Key Choice

At the top of your plot map is the climax, the moment of greatest tension. In terms of your character arc, this is a turning point, when a character is faced with an unavoidable decision. Everything in your story hinges on the climax.

Force your MC to face the source of the conflict head on. Nudge readers to the edges of their seats as the tension reaches its highest point and your MC must rise to the occasion, make key decisions, and face her greatest fear. Release the tension when the outcome of the climactic scene is revealed.

- Battle/fight against prime enemy
- Natural/man-made disaster/weather event
- Ultimatum
- Straw that breaks the camel's back/"Not gonna take it anymore!"
- Key decision
- Facing a fear
- Standing up for herself or others

Falling Action/Processing & Tying Up Loose Ends

Show and tell your main character picking up the pieces from the climax and dealing with whatever new conditions arose out of it. Resolve subplots and allow things to begin returning to normal—even if it's a new normal.

Resolution/What's Next?

Show your main character making plans for the future and settling into the new normal. Show your main character figuring out what she'll do next, now that she's achieved or given up on her objective. Wrap up any remaining loose ends or prep readers for the next installment of the series.

The conflict is resolved when the problem no longer exists. This doesn't mean there's a happy ending, necessarily. It just means the reader knows how things turned out regarding the main conflict.

- Main character achieves objective
- Opposing force stops opposing or goes away
- Main character dies or becomes unable to pursue objective
- Main character gives up, is defeated, or incapacitated
- Main character changes objective
- Main character partially achieves the objective and things return to a relatively calm state, even if there is more to do

Suggested Anchor Scene Writing Recipes
Bulleted List

1. Anchor Scene 1: First Appearance of Protagonist
    a. Where and when does it take place?
    b. Who's in the scene?
    c. What happens?
2. Anchor Scene 2: Inciting Incident
    a. Where and when does it take place?
    b. Who's in the scene?
    c. What happens?
3. Anchor Scene 3: Rising Action*
    a. Where and when does it take place?
    b. Who's in the scene?
    c. What happens?
4. Anchor Scene 4: Decision Leading to Climax
    a. Where and when does it take place?
    b. Who's in the scene?
    c. What happens?
5. Anchor Scene 5: Climax

      a.   Where and when does it take place?

      b.   Who's in the scene?

      c.   What happens?

6.   Anchor Scene 6: Resolution

      a.   Where and when does it take place?

      b.   Who's in the scene?

      c.   What happens?

7.   Anchor Scene 7: Final Scene

      a.   Where and when does it take place?

      b.   Who's in the scene?

      c.   What happens?

*Eventually you're going to have quite a few scenes of rising action. If you have ideas for multiple scenes, that's great–go ahead and create multiple rising action anchor scenes. But don't get overwhelmed by trying to come up with all your rising action right now. One scene, chapter, or event works!

Anchor Scene Table

Anchor Scene	Where? When?	Who's Involved? What Happens?
First Appearance of Main Character		
Inciting Incident		
Rising Action		
Key Decision / Action Leading to the Climax		
Climax		
Resolution of Conflict		
Final Scene		

Example

Anchor Scene	Where? When?	Who's Involved? What Happens?
First Appearance of Main Character	grocery store before dance rehearsal	C & T; establish dancing is legal again
Inciting Incident	dance studio, same day	all 4; flyer about dance competition; solo
Rising Action	March to July	C & T argue about how to prep for dance
Key Decision / Action Leading to the Climax	Calica decides to move past the fear	Aunt Lil, Calica; bulbs bloom
Climax	theater, July; during competition	Calica falls during solo but keeps going
Resolution of Conflict	Day after competition; phone call	C and T make up and appreciate one another
Final Scene	Day after; Calica's backyard	Lost contest; all 4 cats + family and friends

I like to use this table to generate my anchor scenes, not just to store them. Sometimes seeing the container that your ideas need to fill actually prompts you to think of the ideas.

If this structure doesn't make ideas start jumping out of your brain, that's just fine. Remember, this is a way to *organize* your ideas. You have all the ideas from Chapter 4 to *generate* ideas.

Once you know what your anchor scenes will be, add them all to this table or a bulleted list. Then, think about how you'd like to see them as you write. Do you want to use this table as a recipe, or would you feel more comfortable putting your anchor scenes on index cards, sticky notes, a whiteboard, or into a storyboard?

Chapter Check In:
1. Any A-ha! moments from this chapter?
2. What questions did this chapter bring up for you?
3. Anything to add to your Author Toolbox?
4. Do you know enough about your conflict map, character arc(s), and plot hill(s) to create anchor scenes? Use this checklist:
    o Do you know who your protagonist is and what she wants or is trying to accomplish?
    o Do you know your inciting incident? Does it feel realistic within your story?
    o Do you know the resolution of the story–how the conflict will be solved?
    o Do you have an idea of what should happen in the climax that is exciting and that also deeply challenges your protagonist?
5. What are your next steps? If you answered "No" to anything in question 4, go back and re-read Chapter 6: Central Conflict. Then, cruise back through Chapter 4: Finding Your Outlining Style and try out some of the brainstorming methods.

CHAPTER 9: STORY STEPPING STONES

Once you've built anchor scenes, you should be able to see a path from one side of your writing river to the other. The murderous torrent of white water will have calmed to a fast-paced but crossable stretch of water.

But the jumps between those anchor scenes might still be pretty big.

It's time for my favorite part of outlining: the stepping stones that close the gaps between the anchor scene boulders, making your crossing less risky.

What Stepping Stones Do

Stepping stones fill in the gaps of plot and character development between anchor scenes.

When you use stepping stones, you increase the likelihood that you'll make it safely to the other side of your writing river. And you decrease the chances of a big wave of unexpected and problematic plot developments or new story ideas knocking you off balance and into the rushing water. They help you stay focused on your goal and avoid getting overwhelmed.

Stepping stones are also a big help for getting all your great ideas into your story. When inspiration hits and you come up with an event or element you want to include, you can use stepping stone outlining to figure out where it fits in your story.

When to Use Stepping Stone Outlining

In the last chapter you learned how to build key scenes with specific jobs to make sure your story had a sound structure. These scenes needed to be in place before you could really start drafting with gusto. Stepping stone outlining is planning you do ON DEMAND. Yup. You get to pull out this outlining tool anytime you need it.

Stepping stone outlining is looking at where you are in your story, where you want to get next, and creating a plan to get there. You can use it to plan a scene, a chapter, or even a larger sequence, like your falling action.

Use it any time you need more details about your story. It should be your #1 go-to, phone-a-friend solution when you're unsure what to do next. Stuck in the middle of a scene? Wallowing in writer's block? Procrastinating? Stop trying to write and start using stepping stones.

How often you do it is up to you. So are the size and number of stepping stones you create.

Some writers like making giant leaps between one anchor scene and the next. They love the feeling of flying as they're in the air, wondering how they'll make a safe landing on the next known story boulder in the river of writing. They find it thrilling.

Other writers don't care for that uncertainty. They like a lot of small stepping stones between boulders. They like to have each scene clearly laid out so they can step easily from one scene to the other, as if they were walking on solid ground.

And some writers are in between. There are some places where they want a lot of stepping stones in place, maybe for challenging scenes like big fights. But they also enjoy the free feeling of flying sometimes. They don't want to have everything planned out because they often find their best ideas in those airborne moments.

I have a writing client who is a classic Big Picture Thinker. From our very first session, she knew her anchor scenes and the shape of the story she wanted to tell. She's on top of her genre and really clear on her mission statement. But she also loves to write from inspiration, usually in one big burst of energy.

During our sessions, she talks out what her characters will do next from where she left off in the draft. We brainstorm stepping stones based on the character arcs, the plot, and the theme of the story.

But when she sits down to write, she doesn't look at the notes from the session. Instead, she allows her muse to take over. She always gets to the next anchor scene, but not always in the way she had envisioned. It's as if just knowing she has a plan is enough to keep her from getting stuck. It's the perfect combination of flying high and having a safety net.

You'll need to find your own comfort level when it comes to how many stepping stones to create and how closely to follow them. Use stepping stones when you don't know what should happen next or you don't know how to get to your next anchor scene.

If your draft is going along swimmingly, that's wonderful. Keep writing. But if you ever feel "blocked," bust out the stepping stone recipes from this chapter. Remember, the most common cause of writer's block is simply not having a plan!

How to Build Stepping Stones

Take the next plot development you're certain of. Take where you are now. Build a bridge of stepping stones between them.

That might mean working from here to there, asking at every stage, "What would that lead to?" Or you might work from there backwards, asking at every step, "What would have caused that?"

And, of course, you can work from both directions and meet in the middle.

The key is that you're narrowing the scope of possibility and limiting your choices—in a good way. Use questions that spark ideas about your characters, plot, and setting.

- How does the character feel now?
- What does the character want next?
- Why did the character start this activity?
- What will happen if the character doesn't succeed in this moment?
- Who is working against the character?
- What skills does the character have that could be used?
- What flaws does the character have that could cause problems?
- What would motivate the character to do what I need her to?

- What would the character do next if X happened?

Asking these kinds of questions puts you into a problem-solving frame of mind. Instead of waiting for inspiration to strike, you're looking at the current conditions and brainstorming how they could become the conditions you want next.

You already have a lot of useful information about your story from your mission statement, conflict map, and anchor scenes. Stepping stone outlining is using this information to research. You're combing through what you know about your story structure, your characters, and your world, hunting for solutions. This logical approach makes it much easier to figure out your next steps.

You might prefer inspiration, and I get it: That's part of what makes writing fun. Here's the thing, though. If you start with stepping stone thinking, inspiration is going to arrive a lot faster and be a lot more helpful because you'll have primed its pump with a lot of great possibilities.

Stepping Stone Writing Recipes
"Which leads to..." Recipe

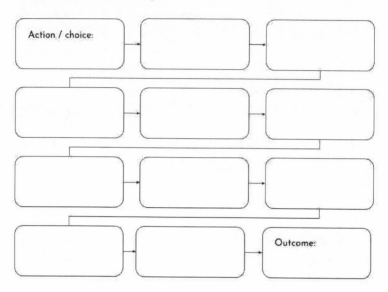

"Which was caused by..." Recipe

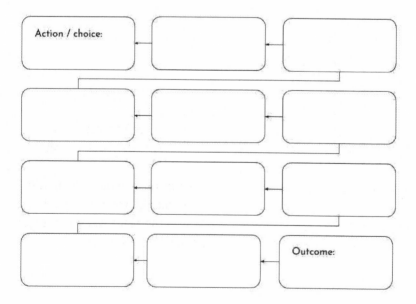

Example

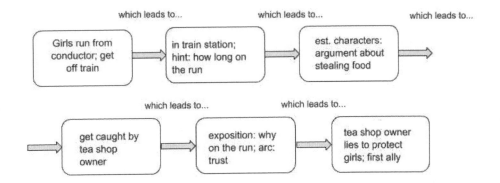

Stepping stones are a system you can use to get answers instead of feeling lost and overwhelmed.

This is also where having a writing coach, community, or buddy is very powerful. You can talk through your stepping stones aloud with someone else who knows your story and characters.

But even on your own, setting your intention and attention to solving a problem is far more effective than staring at the problem and feeling frustrated.

If you can identify the problem, you can troubleshoot it, using the questions above. You can also work on it unconsciously. You might find that if you name the place where you're stuck and the place you want to get to, you'll find yourself dreaming up the solution while you sleep.

Chapter Check In

1. Any A-ha! moments from this chapter?
2. How does this method compare to how you're currently outlining or planning?
3. Anything to add to your Author Toolbox?
4. Do you have enough information to begin using stepping stones? If not, which step do you think you need to go back to? Mission statement? Central conflict? Plot hill? Character arc? Anchor scenes?
5. What are your next steps?

CHAPTER 10: SCENE PLANNING

On our outlining journey from bigger tasks to smaller tasks, we're getting down to the itty bitty.

So far, we've looked at some pretty big pieces, like your big WHY for writing, your central conflict, and the anchor scenes that readers will be expecting.

We just checked out how to fill in stepping stones between those anchor scenes. Once you build those stepping stones, you can see what your scenes might look like. That might mean you can picture them, or it might mean you know the concepts behind them, like knowing a character has to be in some kind of mild danger, but not knowing what that danger will be.

You may not need to go any further for a majority or even for all of your scenes. It really depends on your thinking and writing process.

Some writers can successfully write from their anchor scene recipe and stepping stones, adding in more stepping stones as needed.

I want to introduce you to one more stage of outlining, though, so that you have all the tools you'll need, even if you don't need this last tool all the time. It's like setting the table with a knife, fork, and spoon for every meal. Sometimes you'll just use the fork, but when faced with a steak or a bowl of ice cream, you'll be grateful you have those other utensils.

What Scene Planning Does

Scene planning tells you the must-have ingredients for a given chapter or part of a chapter of your book. It prevents you from:

(1) Over-writing and going down an exposition rabbit hole.

(2) Under-writing and missing key events or character traits.

(3) Pushing the goal posts out and feeling like the more you write, the more there is to write.

(4) Using all TELLs and no SHOWs in your writing.

(5) Endless rewriting and editing.

When to Use Scene Planning

If you know how to start a scene or chapter but can never figure out how to get through the middle bits, or how to tell when it's over, you'll love scene planning.

Wait to create a detailed scene plan until you're about to write that scene in your next drafting session. This part of the planning process gets pretty detailed, so you want to make sure you're using the *right* details.

Try filling out a scene planner well before you sit down to write. The best feeling is if the you-of-the-past fills out a scene planner for the you-of-the-present. That way, the you-of-now can jump in and just draft. That means you won't have to switch from one writing task to another. (Every time you switch, you use up energy in the transition.)

Take five minutes at the end of your writing time today to fill out tomorrow's scene planner. Tomorrow, you can jump in and draft, and at the end of your drafting time take another five minutes to fill out the next day's scene planner, and so on and so on.

You won't necessarily write a scene a day, so use that sequence as a concept rather than a literal recipe.

This system ensures that you've got the most up-to-date intel for your story when you sit down to write, while at the same time protecting you from the mental tug-of-war brought on by trying to plan and draft at the same time.

How to Plan Scenes

The key questions you're asking when using a scene planner are "How will I know when this scene is finished? What are the key elements it needs to have?"

You can define those "key elements" in different terms. Remember those three different approaches to brainstorming I showed you in Chapter 4? Use what works for you:

(1) Do you need to know the nitty-gritty of what's going to happen—the Who, What, Where, When, and How of the scene?

(2) Are you more concerned about Why from the point of view of your characters—their motivations and inner thoughts and feelings based on their arcs?

(3) Or are you more focused on the view from 30,000 feet—where you are in your plot hill and what has to happen to advance the action to the next key anchor scene?

Use what you know about the type of planner you are to jot down notes about your scene. Use as many of the questions below as feel useful:

1. Where will this scene take place?

2. When will this scene take place?

3. What are the most important plot developments/actions that will occur?

4. What are the most important character arc developments that will occur?

5. What seeds do you need to plant now for things that will happen later?

6. What will you show (describe with lots of sensory detail)?

7. What will you tell (summarize)?

Scene Planner Recipe

When? Where?	What Happens?	SHOW not TELL	
		Key Details	Opportunities

Example

When? Where?	What Happens?	SHOW not TELL	
		Key Details	Opportunities
Midnight; behind the elementary school near the woods; cold; spooky night sounds; difference between the country and the city Ronnie's used to	1. Ronnie has to follow through on Dillon's dare to break into the school and steal something 2. R gets caught; D escapes 3. R hears the wolf howl in the woods for the first time	1. R's fear of breaking rules 2.Sheriff's sympathy for R 1. R's growing distrust of D; D's fear of the woods 3. Make the howl really creepy; hint that D knows what's going on but won't say.	1. Ronnie's need to fit in 1. Ronnie's fear of breaking rules 1. Dillon's meanness 3. How scary the woods are and far away from home Ronnie feels

When I filled in this table, I wrote down my ideas as they occurred to me. Then, I went back and added in the numbers so I would know the order I should write it. (Items with the same numbers will go in the same general part of the scene.) This is one of my favorite tricks for creating recipes because it makes it really quick and easy to go from gathering ideas, to arranging them, to being able to draft.

However you do it, taking a few minutes to plan a scene will ensure you include all the key elements necessary for advancing your plot and character arc(s).

Planning scenes is also a great defense against perfectionism because there's an objective way to measure when they're finished. Even if they're not as beautiful as you'd imagined, you can let them be and continue moving forward with your draft.

Chapter Check In

1. Any A-ha! moments from this chapter?
2. What questions did this chapter bring up for you?
3. Anything to add to your Author Toolbox?
4. What are your next steps? If you feel unsure of what a character would do in a scene, try some freewriting. Become the character and freewrite starting with, "I wish..." "I need..." or "I'm afraid..." See what ideas come up.

CHAPTER 11: PUTTING IT ALL TOGETHER

Outlining is serious business. It's the difference between publishing your books and leaving them to languish half-finished on your computer. It relies on rules and formulas, and yet it's incredibly personal. It's a complex system involving many different steps but we often feel the pressure to do it all at once.

With these seemingly contradictory traits, it's no wonder outlining is such a sticky topic for writers. We might all mean something different when we say "outlining," and we might all need very different tools to do this activity effectively.

Let's recap this new approach to outlining so you can see how it will help you write more effectively, and also how you can make each stage of the process work for you.

You saw how beginning with a mission statement grounds your writing in your purpose—your big WHY. Returning to this big why throughout the process of writing your novel will keep you focused. Going in, you'll know everything from your target length to the literary pet peeves that drive you crazy as a reader that you know you want to avoid as a writer.

Anytime you're feeling lost, stuck, or bewildered, dig out your mission statement. Tempted to procrastinate? About to open your favorite social networking site "just to check" what's up? Get inspired by your mission statement!

Taking a little bit of time at the beginning of writing your novel to complete your mission statement will save you countless lost hours later.

You won't get into that "Where am I going and what am I doing" funk that steals time from writers everywhere.

Next, you learned how to construct a central conflict that inspired you and your readers. You figured out where your whole story was going. You saw what was on the far bank, on the other side of your writing river.

Then, you saw how to build anchor scenes to keep you from getting lost on your way to that destination. Once you had those in place, you had the basic shape of your story.

You learned techniques for building smaller stepping stones between those anchor scenes so that you could use analytical thinking and problem-solving to spark your creativity.

Finally, you saw how you could use scene planning whenever you needed more direction for your draft. The scene-planning recipe even helped you determine what you'd describe in great detail so that you could reveal the most important elements of setting, character, and plot.

This six-stage structure works! But maybe you've got some questions about it.

Outlining FAQ

How Far Ahead Should I Plan?

The answer to this depends on your personal writing process. How many scenes in advance do you want to have nailed down before you start writing? Some writers feel lost without a long view. Some writers feel constrained if they plan in detail beyond the very next scene.

Once you have your conflict map and anchor scenes in place, you know where you're headed. If you enjoy the journey more by being spontaneous, start drafting from that point. If you want more of a plan, use the stepping stone and the scene planner recipes to nail down more of your chapters.

How Detailed Does My Outline Need to Be?

How much detail do you need to start writing? Some writers want to be able to imagine everything so they don't miss any key story pieces. Other writers use a sketch to give them the creative freedom they need to get into their "flow" and use what comes to them in the moment.

If you find that your stepping stones or scene planners are turning into complete sentences with description and dialogue, it means you have enough details already in your mind to begin writing. In that case, jump into drafting.

If you're comfortable with just the broad strokes, that's fine. A lot of your stepping stones might be just a glimmer in your eye. But you'll know how to create them when you need them.

The same goes for the scene planners. You've got a secret weapon to use any time the drafting slows down. You'll know you're ready for the next step in outlining when you've gotten what you can from the previous step.

Once again, keep in mind that there are different types of details: the events in the plot; the character motivation; and the behind-the-scenes details you know as the author. Use any or all of those details that help you plan.

I Don't Know What to Write Next. What Should I Do?

Wherever you are in your draft, not knowing what to write next is actually not a problem. The problem is feeling like you must have inspiration in order to move forward. Once you let go of the idea that you're blocked or that your muse left you in the lurch, you can take action to gather the information you need.

This outlining process gives you the tools to discover what you need to know about your story and your characters at every stage.

If you're looking at your anchor scenes but you don't know what to write next, work smaller and create stepping stones. Got a stepping stone in place and still don't know what to write? Fill out a scene planner. Stuck on what to put in your scene planner? Use one of the idea-gathering methods in Chapter 4 to brainstorm.

Reach out to a writing buddy or a coach and explain what question you're trying to answer or what obstacle you're trying to move past. If you can clearly explain the problem, someone can help you solve it.

◆ ◆ ◆

Experiment. Try different methods. Keep track of what works and add it to your Author Toolbox.

Remember that gathering your ideas is often a separate step from putting them into a recipe you can write from.

While some writers can gather their ideas when prompted by a table or graphic organizer or checklist, others will look at those tools and draw a blank. If that's you, make sure you give yourself the space and time to generate ideas in a productive way. Talk it through. Freewrite. Mind map. But don't jump straight to filling out the recipe if it doesn't work for you.

Conversely, if you can write directly from a brainstorm, do it! Don't waste your time creating a recipe if that's not what you need to write.

Let me repeat that because it's hugely important: **I just gave you permission to brainstorm in an outlining template and to draft from a brainstorm.**

I know writers who create a mind map of character connections and conflicts. They color-code that to show where they are in the anchor scenes—one color for the rising action, another for the climax, etc. Then, within each color, they number the ideas to indicate the order of the scenes. (You can give this a try using the Character & Conflict Map template I gave in the resource bundle.)

An outline is simply a plan you can write from. If you can create that plan all in one container, do it. It's like stew in the crockpot.

If you can't, don't force it. The best way to plan and draft your novel is along the path of least resistance. When you do what works for your brain and your thinking style, you'll fight yourself less. You'll get inspired more easily. You'll find yourself sitting at your computer for longer stretches of time before getting fatigued.

I walked you through six stages of outlining that help spark creativity and overcome writer's block. There's one final stage, one last piece of the puzzle: Trusting your unique process. That's what allows you to turn outlining into your trusted friend instead of your archenemy.

When that happens, when outlining is your partner as you write your novel—and it very much is when you use this process and these steps—you get to decide how and when to implement it.

Whatever challenges arise, there is always a step you can take.

At its core, outlining is nothing more than declaring an intention: "This is what I will write and the order in which it will appear in my book."

When you have an effective outline, you don't even have to draft the scenes in the order they will appear. Since you know what leads to what and how it all turns out, you can skip to the exciting parts! Write your climax first. That will motivate you to write the other bits because you know you want your characters to get to that critical moment.

Write the resolution early on and get the hardest scene out of the way.

Start your draft without that terrible pressure of "What's the best opening scene?" Just write your first anchor scene, trusting that as you get deeper into your draft you'll have plenty of great ideas for a killer opening chapter.

The world is your oyster. Your novel is your playground.

The more you plan, the more you can play. Because your process is like a river, too. When you build its banks and send it flowing in the right direction, it can make waves, crash against debris, or rage in roaring rapids—within the confines of its banks. You will still get to where you want to go because you've created a path to success for yourself.

CHAPTER 12: REFLECT & TAKE ACTION

The best way to hold onto new knowledge is to reflect on it—and then to implement it. Begin by answering the questions below. You may want to write down your answers. If you'd like to share any or all of your findings with me, I would love to hear them! You can message me at facebook.com/MeganBarnhardWriting

1. What did you learn from this book?
2. How are you thinking about outlining differently from before?
3. What do you think has been holding you back when it comes to outlining?
4. What's one idea from this book you're ready to try to make outlining more successful for you?
5. What's your motivation? What outcome would you like to see form your increased skills with outlining?

After you reflect, celebrate. I know that might sound a bit odd. Celebrate outlining? Not exactly. What you want to celebrate is taking the time to build your Author Toolbox and invest in your craft. Especially if you've found outlining frustrating in the past.

We all have associations with certain activities. Positive and negative.

You know how your cat hates his carrier? He associates it with going to the vet. Now, of course, you have a much broader understanding of the world than your cat. But if you've been frustrated by outlining in the past, found it limiting, found it ineffectual, or found it to be a big ol' waste of time, some of that residual thinking is still around, even if now you intellectually understand the benefits of outlining. (And I hope you do!)

Since emotions are the shortcuts of the brain—the things that give us an immediate red light or green light about whether to do something—it pays to take a few minutes to create a positive emotional association with outlining. It'll be easier to decide to do it in the future because you'll get an emotional green light instead of an "Oh crap! Not that terrible thing!" kind of message.

Start by rereading your answers to the questions above.

Now close your eyes. (Well, read the rest of this first and then close your eyes so you know what to do once you close your eyes!)

Take a deep breath and feel, right now, how good it feels to improve your writing craft.

With your eyes closed, imagine yourself writing books faster because you now know how to plan them effectively. What will that feel like? What new books are you really excited about writing? What will it feel like to finish them in the next few months instead of in the next few years?

Imagine book royalties coming in. What will it feel like to receive that money? What will you use it for? How will you treat yourself? How will you spoil the people in your life whom you love?

Spend a few minutes in this happy place, visualizing the wonderful things that will happen in your life and in the lives of people (and cats) you care about, all because you have taken the time to learn a new way to outline.

Ahhh...That should feel good.

Don't be shy about rewarding yourself at this point, either. That's always a good way to build a positive association with an activity. New journal and pens, anyone?

Now what?

Well, how about jumping in and starting to outline! Act while this information is still fresh in your mind.

You can download printable versions of all the outline templates we covered in this book over at meganbarnhard.com/outline-recipes

If you really dug this outlining system and you're thinking, "Megan makes this crazy process actually make sense!" I'm happy to continue being your guide. You can learn more about working one-on-one with me—for just a few sessions to get you through a rough patch of your book, or for longer if you want on-going support—at meganbarnhard.com

I love working one-on-one with authors because the more I get to know your story and your writing process, the more I can be a sounding board for all your great ideas, helping you choose what will work best to meet your goals. Plus, I help you discover your best strategies and thinking styles to add to your Author Toolbox.

Take action. USE THIS INFORMATION! It won't do you any good if it's just sitting in your noggin. It will only help your writing process if you really get out there and give it your best go. Go download the outline recipes and start planning! meganbarnhard.com/outline-recipes

If you found this book helpful, you'd make my day if you left a review. Just a few sentences with your honest opinion will help other authors face their outlining fears and get more wonderful books out into the world.

Happy writing,
Megan

ACKNOWLEDGEMENTS

The content of this book wouldn't exist without the hundreds of writers I've coached over the years. Thank you to you all from the bottom of my heart. I can't begin to imagine what it's like to be on the other end of my goofy and often intense teaching and coaching style. I'm forever grateful to your willingness to follow me on the adventure of figuring out writing together.

Thank you to the talented and compassionate tribe of writers I've had the privilege of coaching for the last 11 months. Lloyds and Ladies, you inspire me to no end, and your support means the world to me.

Beth Burnett, Melinda Maxwell-Smith, Carol May Vaughn, Cassidy Taylor, and Lloyd Thompson-Taylor, your comments on the early draft were indispensable. Thank you for being my beta team and helping me make this book more coherent and true to my vision.

I'm hugely indebted to my editor, Lloyd Thompson-Taylor of LTT Editorial Services, for his ability to see through my convoluted sentence structure to the ideas underneath. Thank you for helping me speak as myself rather than to myself. You took amazing care of my book baby, and I'm truly grateful for your energy, compassion, and patience.

Thanks to my hubby who supports me in every way and who ate lots of dinners late and out of the freezer as I did battle with this book. And to Bradbury, who sat on my lap and wouldn't let me get up, no matter how much I wanted to procrastinate.

ABOUT THE AUTHOR

Megan Barnhard is a story magician and writing coach for authors who want to increase productivity, beat writer's block, and sell more books. She specializes in deconstructing the writing process and helping you use all the parts of your writing brain so you can spend more time in your creative flow and less time wanting to throw your laptop out the window in frustration. Megan lives on the Central Coast of California with her husband and their cat Bradbury, who may or may not be the reincarnation of the famous author.

Connect with Megan and learn more about her work with authors:
Website: meganbarnhard.com
Newsletter: meganbarnhard.com/newsletter
Facebook.com/WritewithMegan
Facebook group: Write with Megan

Photo by Gina Cinardo, Ginici Studios

MORE BY THIS AUTHOR

Recipe for Drafting: Beat Writer's Block and Finish the First Draft of Your Novel Faster

Recipe for Storytelling: A Fun & Inspiring Step-by-Step Guide for Telling Your True Story

Could You Live Underwater: A Design Thinking and STEM Curriculum for Curious Learners (co-authored with Jade Rivera; published by Prufrock Press)

The Dancing Cats Compete

Made in the USA
Las Vegas, NV
06 October 2021

31826035R10055